AN OCEAN
Without

| Learning to Embrace Boundaries |

a story in poems
by Sarah Steele

Copyright © 2024 by Sarah Steele
www.bysarahsteele.com

Design and art by James Steele

ISBN 978-0-9974453-3-6 (paperback)
ISBN 978-0-9974453-4-3 (ebook)

Library of Congress Control Number: 2024900466

All rights reserved. No part of this publication may be reproduced, stored in a retrieval system, or transmitted in any form by any means—electronic, mechanical, photocopying, recorded or other—except for brief quotations in reviews, without permission from the author.

Email permission requests to stuffbysarahsteele@gmail.com.

All Scriptures are quoted, unless otherwise indicated, are from the NET Bible® http://netbible.com copyright ©1996, 2019 used with permission from Biblical Studies Press, L.L.C. All rights reserved.

Scripture quotations marked (ESV) are from The ESV® Bible (The Holy Bible, English Standard Version®), © 2001 by Crossway, a publishing ministry of Good News Publishers. Used by permission. All rights reserved.

Scripture quotations marked (NIV) are taken from the Holy Bible, New International Version®, NIV®. Copyright © 1973, 1978, 1984, 2011 by Biblica, Inc.™ Used by permission of Zondervan. All rights reserved worldwide. www.zondervan.com. The "NIV" and "New International Version" are trademarks registered in the United States Patent and Trademark Office by Biblica, Inc.™

To James: who carried me when I fell

Three Meals a Day

He made breakfast every morning.
I was not sleeping well—
the baby, the heartache.
If I did get up before the littles,
I desperately wanted to read my Bible—
or at least sit and stare.
So he woke up with time enough
and made breakfast every morning.

He made lunch every noon.
I was always nursing
or correcting or crying.
If I did have time to stand on my own,
I desperately wanted to take a shower—
or at least hide in the bathroom.
So he took a break from work
and made lunch every noon.

He made dinner every evening.
I was so tired from having existed all day
and protecting my mind from itself.
If I did have energy to make food,
I desperately wanted it to be muffins—
or at least tea and honey.
So he returned from his full day at work
and made dinner every evening.

Dear Reader,

The following words recount
a difficult period in my life;
my slavery to doing good deeds
had only reaped a harvest of strife.
When I finally came to a bitter end
and found I had injured many friends,
heart started to shake and then descend—
it was clear I was losing the fight.

The rest of the story includes
anxiety I had never known;
deep sorrow pervaded all through me,
right down to my very bones.
But through tear-filled counseling and God's true Word
and friends who ever-so-gently spurred,
a rebuilding began as had never occurred—
with Christ as my Cornerstone.

If you want to talk about boundaries
or personal limits God has placed,
if you want to discuss codependency
and whole selves being erased,
if anxiety's pressing hard on your mind,
or people-pleasing's put you in a bind—
take care and come close; we are of the same kind.
These words will grow us in grace.

♡ Sarah

CHAPTERS

Swimming | 2

Drowning | 42

Rescued | 84

Weeping | 130

Floating | 164

PROLOGUE

Redeemed I

I used to love and serve
and give sacrificially.

It made me feel
good and worthy.

But one day,
my love was not enough;
my service was unwanted;
and the sacrifice was me.

It made me feel
broken and useless
and very afraid.

Today I love and serve
and give sacrificially.

And I don't feel anything
but gratitude to God.

This book is the story
of what happened
in between.

chapter one
Swimming

fear of insignificance

i became friends with
people who needed me,
to whom i would not be
expendable.

empathy

i see your pain and
hear your pain and
feel your pain
in the depths of my soul.

i'm not sure how i
can sustain your
life with mine,
but i'll try to control

the pain you feel and
the pain you hold and
the pain that's
coursing through your life.

i'll be there for you;
i'll see you through,
and you won't bear alone
one more moment of strife.

come to me,
all you who are weary
and heavy-laden,
and i will give you rest.

—only Jesus should say that

lies i tell my friends

i am big enough
for all your problems.

out of my way

i am an endless source
of energy and
helpfulness;
i identify problems
and enact solutions.
no consultation
necessary.

—you're welcome

the helper's high

inhale the air of needs

    exhale nervous energy

inhale others' pain

    exhale mounting anticipation

inhale a plan to help

    exhale the assistance

inhale their gratitude

    exhale—and look for more

Needy Servant

You don't have to say a thank-you.
(I might crumble if you don't.)
You don't have to see my service.
(I won't be hurt—I won't.)
Maybe I should serve you longer
or louder for a time;
I'd just hate for you to miss me
while I'm in my service prime.

Yes

Yes, I'll hear your fears
and offer help;
you don't need to implore me.

Yes, I'll text you back
with hours of thought;
it's okay if you ignore me.

Yes, I'll wash your clothes
and clean your house
and scrub your dishes too.

Yes, I'll gather
other helpers up;
it's the least that I can do.

Yes, I'll give you milk
I pumped myself,
while I eat your special diet.

Yes, I'm sorry that
I once complained;
I'm thrilled you made me try it.

Yes, I'm "here to serve,"
I "aim to please,"
and all those other isms.

(I just can't say no
and open myself up
to criticism.)

good girls don't swear

boundaries is the
christian b-word,
and i want nothing
to do with them.

but a friend says
boundaries
are important,
so i roll my eyes
and give it a whirl.

i tried || boundaries: take one

um hi!
how are ya?
oh not great?
tough day?
ugh, i'm sorry to hear that;
that's really terrible.
so this probably isn't a good time,
but i was thinking about
stepping back and
helping juuuust a little bit less
and was wondering—
what's that?
oh, things are actually getting worse for you,
and really, if anything, you need more?
of course!
how thoughtless of me!
how selfish!
no, no, it's really no trouble.
i'd love to keep it up.
i mean, truly, it's a gift to ME
to serve in this way.
how 'bout this:
whenever you're ready for less,
you let me know,
and i'll stay over here
plugging away until then.
of course!
don't give it another thought.
love you;
hope tomorrow's better!

close call

stomach tightens
then releases
with the conflict
just avoided.
giving people
what they ask for
isn't like being exploited.
it's just helping me
to be less selfish
when my needs are voided.

disappointing others
is worse than
disappointing myself.

                                              for if you're disappointed,
                                                  surely God is too.

shutting down

i know about anger,
know how to be bitter,
am constantly frustrated,

but

these heart palpitations
are brand-new sensations—
seems safer to keep my heart

shut.

numb

i live in a constant
state of denial—
nothing hurts;
nothing's wrong;
i am fine.

relationships are painful;
tasks are rewarding.

—*stay busy*

last one caring

must be nice
to look at
someone's need
and turn away.

must be nice
to know
your "plate is full,"
no more to say.

must be nice
to laugh
while someone else
lives in mayhem.

good thing i'm here
to demonstrate
true selflessness
to them.

—somebody give me credit

God helps those
who help other people.

—1 Sarah 3:15

betrayed

burdens i carry
are neither easy nor light;
i am being crushed.

limitless

lacking limits

        does not make me patient

lacking limits

        does not make me kind

lacking limits

        does not make me generous

—it makes me resentful

mother, may i?

mother, may i help you?
mother, may i give
my bank and mind
and love combined
to help your life to live?

except you're not my mother,
and i'm already wearing thin.
yet still i bend,
your needs attend;
i want to help you win.

codependency

icanttellwhereiend
andyoubeginandi
thinkitfeelsgoodto
besoentangledeven
thoughiknowsome
thingisnotquiteright

trying again || boundaries: take two

hey there!
how are you?
oh, not great.
tough day again?
ugh, i'm so sorry, that's a bummer.
you need some help?
i'm sorry, but
i, uh, can't do that.
you really need it?
oh, well, actually, sorry, i'm busy.
you don't mind if it's later?
well, um, it's just that i don't know how.
it's really easy?
oh, well, i'm sorry i can't;
i hope you find someone!
you have?
you're bringing it over right now?
but, um, i can't,
i mean,
i guess, i don't
reallyhaveanythingelsetodoanyway.
yep.
see you soon.

black hole

when gravity
is so strong
that light
cannot escape

uneducated

she asked me if i
wanted to help.

i didn't,
so i said,

yes

because i didn't know
any other words.

just keep helping

i was so afraid
my *no* would negate
all the work i had done
that i just—couldn't—stop.
i thought *this*
was the good deed
that would be
remembered,
that would turn
things around.

yes or no

if i can't say no,
then i should not mumble yes;
with freedom comes choice.

i'm not okay
when you're not okay.

—*codependency is slavery*

abandonment

if i tell you no,
will you leave me too?

Galatians 1:10a

Am I now trying to gain the approval of people, or of God? Or am I trying to please people?

obsessed

my eyes follow you around the room,
trying to determine if you are pleased,
if i can rest.

i jump at your needs
as much for my own comfort
as for yours.

my eyes glance at phone,
trying to discern if you are disappointed,
if i am enough.

i offer proactively before you demand
as much for my own relief
as for yours.

following the star

i agreed to the help
i had begged to give.
pick me, pick me;
this is why i live.

when you changed the terms
and asked that i
do more with less,
i didn't care why.

just bent a little farther,
fit under your bar.
just beat my body harder
to follow your star.

bad idea

here i am—cosigning on your life
and paying all your debts,
while you've quit your job
and are off on vacation.

idolatry

i sacrificed my body
on the altar of your needs.
that makes you my idol
and me your worshiper.

to be all

i tried to be

    e v e r y t h i n g

you needed
and wanted,

but in the end,

my head was wind,
my body waves,
and my legs stone.

turns out i became

    e v e r y t h i n g ,

which left me with
nothing at all.

surprise emotions

innocent story,
being shared
by sister who
shows she cares.

but suddenly,
she's forced to stop;
she looks up sharp
and sees me sob.

i don't understand
these things i feel;
i'm embarrassed that
i couldn't conceal

the painful bits
inside my heart.
i dry my eyes,
and she restarts.

faulty interpretation

you bear my burden;
i'll carry your load.
that's the way
the scripture goes.
but how to do that
i don't know.
so i begin to
overload
and friend-bulldoze,
keep face composed,
don't dare expose,
yes, please impose!
until i finally implode,
and slowly, next i
decompose,
while rows of
heart-shaped dominoes
fall shattered there
upon the road.

natural disaster

an ocean
without a boundary
is a catastrophe.

chapter two

Drowning

i'm sorry

i
can't
do
this
any
more.

an explanation

when i said i couldn't help anymore,
i meant that i'm not even able
to take care of myself right now.

when i said i was sorry,
i meant that i was so foolish
to tell you to rely on me alone.

backlash

eyes so pointed
they pierce
right through me;
tongue so sharp
i bleed.

heart stops beating;
next moment i
collapse,
no longer plead.

suffocating

can you vomit if
you can't even breathe?

service interrupted

the first time
i couldn't lift my arms
was the beginning
of learning
how to serve
with my heart.

spinning out

everywhere i turn,
(i'm sure) heads shake slowly
in pitiful disgust.
she tried her best, they scorn.
and it was not enough.
it has never been enough.

feeling

i used to live in
a constant state
of denial,
but now
everything hurts,
everything's wrong,
and i am falling apart.

No

No, I can't go back
to the way things were,
but I can't move forward either.

No, I won't pretend
that I'm all right;
I'm taking my first breather.

No, you can't come in
and take my hand
and pray us back to better.

No, I can't say more;
my words are gone
in the bottom of life's shredder.

notifications

every signal
        every ding
                every bell
                      and every ring
                            makes me jump
                          my heart racing
                  and so i turn
        alert settings
to off

locked doors

i never used to lock my doors
when i was home alone.
kind neighbors and the dearest friends
are all i've ever known.

but now i'm filled with so much fear,
i lock and bolt all doors
and flinch at every passing car,
afraid it might be yours.

reaching out

hi mom,
i uh need help.
    i can't breathe;
    i can't think.
could i come?
could you watch the kids?
you will?

hi dad,
i uh
don't think i can drive
    because i can't
    lift my arms.
could you—
you will?

breathing

the littles are gone;
the baby is dozing.
i'm looking around;
my heart is still frozen
       in fear—

            so i breathe.

i stare out the window
and look at cows munch
over there in the field
as they quietly lunch
       without fear—

            and i breathe.

i gaze at the clouds
floating peacefully by.
i know nothing of peace;
all i know is that i'm
       filled with fear—

            but i breathe.

siblings

i was born first.
crawled first,
walked first,
fell
      first.

and yet somehow,
it was the babies, who

heard my cries
and came running, who

gasped at my condition
and wiped my tears, who

stood in a hedge around me
while finding all my pieces, who

picked me up and carried me back—
whole.

conversation with my four-year-old

are you going to sit and read and not talk all day?
yes, but only for another day or two.
then you will be the mom again?

empowered

i drive through countryside,
manually shift into each gear.
i tell that car exactly when
and where it should go.
and it does.

going home

the time to return
is here, and i fill with dread
at the things to come.

they're there

i hug my parents,
choke on sobbing gratitude;
then i say goodbye.

what my neighbor saw

"the curtains on the red house across the street
used to be open from dawn 'til dark.
a glance inside revealed love and laughter and
'welcome! come on in!'

"but one day the curtains closed,
the music stopped echoing out the window, and
but for the occasional glimmer of peeking light,
they disappeared from our street altogether."

Psalm 69:1–3

Deliver me, O God, for the water has reached my neck. I sink into the deep mire where there is no solid ground; I am in deep water, and the current overpowers me. I am exhausted from shouting for help. My throat is sore; my eyes grow tired from looking for my God.

friends who show up

you came
when no one else came.

you asked
when no one else
even knew the question.

you listened
when i fumbled with words.

you were unafraid
when emotions loomed large.

i cried in a corner on the couch,

and you came
and asked
and listened
and were unafraid.

—how can i ever thank you

deeper in

i long for silence,
for space enough to hear,
but the chill and the children
shove me deep inside,
until it is just my thoughts,
loud and unorganized as they are.

and so i have to practice the
discipline of fighting my own mind,
so that God's whisper can make its way
into my heart.

accepted

my neighbor waves from
her front yard, and
my body walks
across the street.

all it takes is one compassionate
how are you?
for tears to come to my eyes.

i don't have many words yet, but
i do know i'm not okay.

she dances beautifully between
sensitive questions and
knowing gestures and
neither requires anything of me
nor avoids me.

i feel seen;
i feel not-too-much;
i feel relief.

not forever
—by future me

it hurts,
and you can't stop shaking,
and you swear you won't make it through,
and you'll never trust again,
but you will,
        and you will,
                and you will.

adrenal fatigue

i pour my coffee down the drain.
my cup is already overflowing with
        warm liquid spilling from eyes,
        heart made dark by grief,
        bitter regrets,
        and ripples of anxiety
        that stain every side.

silent

i long to write.

i have something to say,
but my words seem lost.

big feelings swirl,
but just round and round,
never down, never out.

maybe someday
my pen will find
its way
again.

conversation

whenever the ball was passed,
whether to me or someone else,
i'd take it and dribble circles
around players,
up and down the court.

but now,
i hide behind teammates,
pray the ball doesn't come to me,
and pass it off as soon
as it touches my hands.

i hope someday
i'll love to play
again.

to-do list

- ☐ storytime at the park: smile at other moms; be present with kids

- ☐ pick up milk: keep eyes and mind on road

- ☐ host playdate: ~~don't dump woes all over friend~~

- ☐ apologize for dumping woes all over friend

- ☐ hide at home after embarrassing social faux pas

- ☐ stew on general horribleness of self

- ☐ visit chiropractor/vitamin specialist/massage therapist (somebody can make me feel better!)

- ☐ do something (anything!) for someone (anyone!): i am still an important, contributing, significant, worthy, helpful, meaningful member of this world (right?)

- ☐ ~~don't think about potential interactions at church~~

- ☐ throw up after thinking about potential interactions at church

- ☐ go to church: keep coat on (extra layer of protection), walk straight to seat, don't make eye contact with anyone who might ask how i am

- ☐ try not to cry at small group

- ☐ KEEP IT TOGETHER, WOMAN

on writing and being alone

extroverts need to process *externally*,
but i had far too much to say
and was far too afraid of others
to do any of that processing
with another human.
*and please, counseling is for
people who have truly suffered.*
(one day i would recant this.)

so every saturday morning,
i left the house
in search of quiet
to read my bible and
self-therapy book of choice,
*since i can do this myself
thankyouverymuch.*
(one day i would recant this too.)

and then i would write.

i filled two journals
during those saturdays
with prayers
and psalms
and copious notes,
and as i emptied myself,
God began to fill me with
a mustard seed of his peace
and the slightest understanding
of his enduring love.

but

reading therapy
is not a full substitute
for face-to-face help.

it's not working

                                                    i

                                        find

                                 myself

                          at the edge

                    of my own mind,

            waiting to be pushed off

           this mountain of safety and

           sanity. i wish i were between

         that rock and hard place, but

     instead, i am about to free fall to

    my demise, and as i peer over the

ledge, i feel your finger on my back.

                                         —here i go

Psalm 55:4-5, 12-14

My heart beats violently within me; the horrors of death overcome me. Fear and panic overpower me; terror overwhelms me.

Indeed, it is not an enemy who insults me, or else I could bear it; it is not one who hates me who arrogantly taunts me, or else I could hide from him. But it is you, a man like me, my close friend in whom I confided. We would share personal thoughts with each other; in God's temple we would walk together among the crowd.

panic attack

i want to tell you something about anxiety.

you might think it's just about
being nervous and cautious,
but that's far too sweet and mild.
can you close the eyes of
your assumptions
for just a moment
and walk with me along this ocean?
this beautiful, powerful ocean.

you see it, right?

with waves crashing in the distance,
seagulls chattering overhead,
children playing,
grown-ups strolling,
until the dark thunder clouds
come rolling in in an instant.
the picnic baskets get closed up,
the people scatter,
and even the birds find their way home,
until there's nothing but us,
watching from the cliff above the shore,
watching the whitecaps rise higher,
watching the beach shrink.

but wait.
this is too kind,

because we are actually on the beach,
and the determined waves are hammering the shore,
and the thunder is roaring,
and we've been shoved apart by the wind,
our shouts nearly inaudible over its deafening booms.

but hold on.
this is still inadequate,

because we are actually in that ocean,
separated by crashing waves,
dipping under, rising above,
grasping for any little thing.
there are no screams loud enough to bring help.
can God hear prayers spoken only in your mind?

except that it's still not quite right,

because the ocean and the storm are actually inside of you,
while you are lying in your bed
or sitting on your couch
with your friends or your family,
in safe places like the grocery store or church,
and the waves keep pounding down your lungs,
every gulp, more liquid than oxygen,
and the scariest part is that you look safe,
you seem okay,
and nobody can see that you're drowning from the inside out.

this is what bad days with anxiety are like.
i just wanted you to know that.

Psalm 38:6-22

I am dazed and completely humiliated; all day long I walk around mourning. For I am overcome with shame, and my whole body is sick. I am numb with pain and severely battered; I groan loudly because of the anxiety I feel. O Lord, you understand my heart's desire; my groaning is not hidden from you. My heart beats quickly; my strength leaves me. I can hardly see. Because of my condition, even my friends and acquaintances keep their distance; my neighbors stand far away. Those who seek my life try to entrap me; those who want to harm me speak destructive words. All day long they say deceitful things…I am like a man who cannot hear and is incapable of arguing his defense. Yet I wait for you, O Lord! You will respond, O Lord, my God! I have prayed for deliverance, because otherwise they will gloat over me; when my foot slips they will arrogantly taunt me. For I am about to stumble, and I am in constant pain. Yes, I confess my wrongdoing, and I am concerned about my sins. But those who are my enemies for no reason are numerous; those who hate me without cause outnumber me. They repay me evil for the good I have done; though I have tried to do good to them, they hurl accusations at me. Do not abandon me, O Lord. My God, do not remain far away from me. Hurry and help me, O Lord, my deliverer.

a heavy load to carry

i carry anxiety
in my heart
        when it thuds
        and drops
        and races.

i carry anxiety
in my arms
        when i can't lift
        and power
        debases.

i carry anxiety
in my mouth
        when i feel such
        unquenchable
        thirst.

i carry anxiety
from my head
to the ground;
        i'm afraid
        i am forever
        cursed.

approached

someone came up to me today and asked
if she could help me with my problem.

i freaked out (in my mind; i'm still too
humiliated to say what i mean).

how does she know about my problem, or
what problem does she think i have?

with whom has she spoken, and did they tell the
whole truth, and now all i want is to speak my side
of the story, but my mouth is frozen in fear, like
when you try to scream or run in a nightmare, but
nothing comes out and your body won't move.

i accept the book she offers
with shame and resignation.

so this is what it's like
for someone to assume
they know how to fix you.

dear diary

we haven't hosted in a while.
i hate how unavailable i am
for smiles and
other people right now, so
when the missionary asked
to share a meal,
we felt we couldn't say no.

i think i've forgotten how
to be hospitable, though.
because i burned the food,
all the kids cried,
and i tried to listen—
i really tried—
but my eyes saw fuzzy gray,
and my ears only picked up
static-y haze.

so i took the baby upstairs
and returned in time
to say goodbye.

—now it's my turn to cry

invisible

i'm afraid you see me
and you know,
or you see me
and *think* you know,
or maybe i'm afraid that
you don't even see me
at all.

s a c r e d

feet flying
legs gliding
heart pumping
lungs expanding
eyes receiving
mind clearing

stranger coming

mind alerting
eyes darting
lungs heaving
heart racing
legs burning
feet pounding

s c a r e d

i am in the store
and turn around
to feel a fist
connecting with my face and
hands encircling my neck, and
i am on the floor,
gasping for breath, when
i shake my head and see
my steering wheel and realize—
i haven't left the car yet.

—visions are not reality, visions are not reality

chapter three

Rescued

basement counseling

i was attached to my house by
a rope of fear and a nursing babe,
so when i asked for help in a whisper breathed
through telephone wire, she came tiptoeing
through my door and met me underground.

therapy

"so tell me what's going on," she prods,
and tear by sorrowful tear,
my broken heart comes further out
of my heaving chest.
she holds it gently,
pressing a few cracks together
while she listens.

ninety minutes later,
i am out of both tears and words,
and still she sits there
massaging my heart.
"i bet that felt good to get out," she comments,
as she passes it back to me
for safekeeping until next week.
and that was my first counseling session.

Mantra I

"I need Thee every hour,"
in grocery stores,
while cleaning floors,
and when I'm in the shower.

"I need Thee every minute,"
when teaching math,
and giving baths,
and with my newfound limits.

"I need Thee every second,"
when making lunch,
with shoulders hunched,
and fears start fresh to threaten.

—God, please help me

It's My Turn to Talk

She passes the ball to me, and I self-consciously give a brief reply, before lobbing it back in her direction with an embarrassed, "I'm sorry I held that so long." But the ball comes right back without apology or shame, with a request to stick around for a while. I hold it curiously, feel my fingers digging in, notice heat rising (in the ball or in my face?), and quickly toss it back. She walks the ball over to me, places it into my lap, and says, "It might feel uncomfortable when you first hold it. But then it feels really, really good. Just sit with it for now. I don't need this ball today." And so, with fingers trembling, I begin to lightly roll it around in my hands, bounce rubber against floor, until a rhythm of words—angry and aching, gasping and breaking—leave my mouth and, subsequently, my heart, ricocheting off wood paneling and drop ceiling, eyes closed, hand trying to remember how to find the ball by feel, how to find words without fear. I couldn't play with others yet, but it was a start.

verbal vomit

please help catch my words—
they're coming too fast, and i
don't have a bucket.

my counselor

might see my hair stylist,
who might see the neighborhood grocer,
who might see our favorite librarian,
who might see that one mom from the park,
who might see my chiropractor,
who might see my best friend,
who might see my pastor,
and just by looking,
they'll all know that
i'm messed up.

confused

i asked someone
for help today.

they said *no*.

i didn't know
you could do that,

and i can't decide
how i feel about it.

second-guessing

i'm sorry for wasting your time
with my silly, insignificant needs.
please don't spend one more resource on me;
save it for those truly suffering.

delusions

i smiled today and realized that
my troubles are finally over, and i'm fully well,
all thanks to my counselor and husband and God.
phew, that could've been much worse.

the next day

i went to the store and kept
staring at ingredient labels,
wondering who i would disappoint
if i purchased this one or that.

i didn't realize how long i'd been
standing there, until i noticed that
my heart was racing and tears
were streaming down my face.

i didn't think *soap* would be the thing that
triggered all the fear i've been storing up.

—so i guess it's not over

all mixed up

i've been practicing my *no* lately. it makes me feel NERVOUS that others won't understand or approve of my choices, but then i feel MAD that i'm nervous, which makes me feel INFERIOR to others' opinions and then OUTRAGED at their apparent with-it-ness.

—i need a timeout

other people's boundaries

my *no* was ignored for so long that
it disappeared from my mouth and
replaced itself with a toddler.

now when someone tells me *no*,
i want to throw myself on the floor
and kick and scream:

NO ONE is allowed to use that word!

mean

i don't know how
to say what i mean
without being mean
and sounding mean
and feeling mean.

tantrum || boundaries: take three

hello?
um hey,
i'm fine.
what's up?
you need something?
you NEED something?
you seriously NEED SOMETHING
AND YOU'RE CALLING ME?
ME!
THE ONE WITH THE NEWBORN AND TODDLER AND
PRESCHOOLER AND KINDERGARTENER—
ME!
THE ONE WITH DEBILITATING ANXIETY—
ME!
THE ONE WHO STILL CAN'T GO TO THE GROCERY STORE
WITHOUT CRYING OVER SOAP? (SOAP!)
ME!
THE ONE WHO CAN'T GO TO CHURCH WITHOUT SHAKING,
WHO'S NOT SLEEPING AT NIGHT, WHO ISN'T EVEN MAKING
MEALS FOR MY OWN FAMILY YET, WHO CAN'T SMILE OR
HOST OR CHIT CHAT OR WALK WITHOUT LOOKING
OVER MY SHOULDER OR EVEN SIT IN SILENCE, BECAUSE
SILENCE IS THE SCARIEST PLACE TO BE WITH A MIND
IN THIS CONDITION, BUT THAT DOESN'T MEAN I NEED
YOUR PROJECT TO KEEP IT BUSY.
wow.
that felt amazing.
okay, what were you calling about?
hello?

stay away!

a friend asks how i'm doing today.
my husband touches my arm with care.
don't talk to me!
don't touch me!

—intimacy is vulnerability is pain

corporate prayer

he invites me to pray with the group.
i walk to the back of the room and
pretend my baby needs care.

—prayer is intimacy too

Best

Do people
really do their
best?
I want to
scream, "No!"
But I'm afraid
the answer
is yes.

she was everything i was
and nothing i am.

—i'm jealous of my past self

hiding

i withdrew inside my mind,
like a caterpillar stuffing itself
inside its cocoon with no intention
of ever transforming.

butterflies came by,
inviting me to emerge—
some insisting,
others reaching for my hand.

many kindnesses were dismissed
during my self-consumed days of agony,
though a few were victorious
in getting an antenna to peek out
or a whisper returned.

unplanned guide

you never planned how you'd respond
in someone else's darkest hour.
you maybe couldn't even see
the depths of shadows in my bower,
with your own light shining brightly
as i, in the corner, cowered.

and yet, you recognized my anguish,
walked so gently alongside me,
taking in your hand my own,
your light now blazing, there to guide me
back to Jesus; finally feeling
darkness leaving, spark inside me.

tea bag sisters

they say boiling water
just pulls out what is
already in the tea bag.

but what if the tea bag
is a mediocre friendship,
filled with misunderstandings
and differing personalities
packaged together in obligation?

how is it possible that
when boiling water
came pouring down on us,
you came seeping out with love
that covered my bitterness and
filled my cup with steadiness
and understanding
and strength
and hugs?

—you were my friend; now you're my sister

predictions

i'm afraid of
being afraid,
and every time
i feel okay,
i'm sure that
not-okay is
coming soon.

some days

some days i feel just fine,
and some days are the worst.
some days i'm certain i will die,
then hope is interspersed.

some days my faith is waning;
some days it feels stronger.
and some days i am certain
i can't do this any longer.

kindness,
graciousness,
gentleness,
patience—
all given to a friend in need.

so why the
judgment,
critique,
self-shame
when the needy soul is me?

—be kind to yourself

Dayenu

A little word I knew it not,
but once I heard I never forgot.
It seared my soul with iron hot—
dayenu means enough.

I chose to write it on my skin,
remind my heart where it has been,
lest I fall prey to lies again.
It means more than enough.

It's rested there for nigh a year,
pulsating out with message clear,
when just today an ache drew near
that said, "It's not enough."

My heart was longing for some thing;
true happiness I thought it'd bring.
Fast to my dream I strove to cling,
so I could have enough.

Then I glanced down toward feet on floor
and heard my heart say, "I am poor,"
but read the message there once more
and asked, "What is enough?"

It's not enough to change my lot.
It's not enough to hope and plot.
It's not enough to stew on oughts.
I'LL NEVER HAVE ENOUGH!

And with that declaration blurt,
that word reached in, Truth to assert.
It started work to heal the hurt.
There's only one Enough.

"Enough I am," my Lord replied.
"Enough it was for you I died.
Enough it is I call you Bride.
In me, you have Enough."

Enough? My heart knows not this word.
Enough? Indeed, my vision's blurred.
But that's his voice I'm sure I heard.
I know his love for me's endured.
It's in his hand I am secured.
I'll rest in his Enough.

heart work at the park

i'm here at the park,
working hard on my heart,
when two women walk up,
and they talk from the start
with the usual chit-chat
of *hi* and *how are...*
i deflect and just hope
that they'll go away far.

when one asks if she
could quick pray for my work,
and i think that refusing
would make me look like a jerk.
so she starts and my heart squirms
and wants hard to shirk.
when all of a sudden,
my spirit deep stirs,
and i notice a change
in the words that are hers.

and i sense that God's Spirit
has spoken just now,
and i sneak a small look,
though my head is still bowed.
i feel some resistance;
will i yet allow?
but the Spirit is stronger
and breaks through somehow.

tears rush down my face;
i can no longer brace
for the impact of Love
that is here in this place.

and i know that my God
has met me at this table,
and i know that he loves me,
and i know he is able
to heal me completely.
i breathe in and am stable.

Jesus Prays for Me

Jesus prays for me.
This I know,
for the Bible
tells me so.
Little Self,
to him you belong;
when you are weak,
he is strong.

nighttime storms

i pray myself to sleep,
soothing violent seas
with promise of peace,
but any slight disturbance
brings the waves shooting out
with volcanic force,
taunting me to attempt
to lull them again.

breaths of prayer

all i know to pray is
please, make this stop.
but i learn to pray
please, help me endure.

on meditation

breathe in

        gather mental chaos

breathe out

        release swirling thoughts

breathe in

        consider a sacred line

breathe out

        soak in its truth

breathe in

        and know that God

breathe out

        is here with you

breathe in

        you need nothing more

breathe out

practicing the presence of God

my silence is in him;
my thinking is with him;
my questions are to him;
my writing is for him.

if an addict

needs his drugs and his source / and can only think
of her next hit / or if his supply is running low / if she
is irritated with those she claims to love / if he will do
anything—even inappropriate things—to be happy / if
she attracts a particular kind of person / and he needs
support to change / then i think you understand a little /
of what it is to be / emotionally dependent

course corrections: one

i swerve wildly,
zig zag across the road,
occasionally collide with
an oncoming car.
i feel battered, high-strung,
and afraid to keep driving.
but this car is moving
(or maybe the road is),
so i have no choice but
to steer, albeit in awkward,
jerky, effortful motions.

inedible

my insides are churning,
replaying conversations
of the day:
i'm a loser;
they're a jerk.
i didn't mean;
they didn't understand.
up and down,
push and pull,
until i look beneath
to see if all this work
has at least left me with
some butter.

—anxiety is not nutritious

anxiety comes out

sometimes it looks like
waking up drenched
in the middle of the night
from holding it clenched
inside my belly.

sometimes it looks like
insatiable thirst
all the day long
from breathing outbursts
unawares in the night.

sometimes it looks like
a racing heart
during kitchen chores,
mind existing apart
from my body.

and sometimes it looks like
sweat dripping down
while pedaling fast,
grin coming from frown
in being proactive.

how will i let my
anxiety come out?

because it will.

stuck

i hurt you with my *no*.
i wish i could take it back,
except my *yes* was hurting me.
it feels the odds are stacked
against us both, and so we now
sit stewing in our pain.
maybe soon with vision cleared,
we won't the other blame?

exhausted

i spend my waking hours
wrestling fears into cages,
my hands the only locks.

but as i ease into unconsciousness,
my grip loosens, and come dawn,

they have all surrounded me
once again, ready to pounce
at the first flicker of my eyelids.

Mantra II

My

        heart is racing
        wave is rising
        mind is drowning

Grace

        to get up
        to speak up
        to ease up

Is

        God near?
        all life fear?
        anyone here?

Sufficient

        is he
        today for me
        to be free

For

        my good and
        his glory

You

        can rest
        in God's grace
        alone

introductions: part one

my counselor finally uses the word
codependent,
and my cheeks flush hot.

i don't know what it means,
but it sounds like a "thing," and
what happened to me is terrible
and unique and not something
to be looked up in a dictionary with
a clean explanation alongside it.
my heart is too broken and messy
to be defined in a single word, and
i want to reject it entirely, except
somewhere in my bones, i know—

I KNOW—

she is right.

i read one book and then another,
face burning with shame and
indignation, until finally, it is only
my tears that can cool this fever.

i'm not unique.
i'm not special.
but also.
i'm not alone.
and there's a way out.

introductions: part two

when you see someone but
don't know their name or
their values or behaviors,
you might feel intimidated
or nervous.

you don't know
if they are kind
or helpful
or are looking
to destroy you.

but once you are introduced
and learn a little of each other,
you have the knowledge and
power to choose how to
move forward or part ways.

—that's how i feel about naming addictions

Something's Broken

I thought I had a broken arm
from falling down so hard.
So when I asked for help,
I didn't need to dig too far.

"It hurts right here," I pointed.
"I only need a sling
to give it time to heal, so I
can get back into things."

My doctor looked with knowing
and shook her head so sweetly.
"I'd like to run some other tests
to see you more completely."

I rolled my eyes and let her try,
and then I made her pause.
"I have no need to see much more;
I know my pain's true cause."

And so a few more months went by,
and still I had not healed.
I returned then to my doctor
with one final appeal.

"What's happening? Why does it hurt?
Why am I still not well?
I have a life to live here, and
I don't have time to dwell."

My doctor held the x-ray
she had taken from the start,
and I gasped and stumbled when I saw
not arm, but broken heart.

chapter four

Weeping

broken

i thought
i had
been broken;
turns out
i always
was.

obligations

compulsive service
feigns a heart posture of love
whose true root is pride.

rotten roots

the pernicious seeds of arrogance
and pride and self-sufficiency
when left untended don't die,
but rather grow deeper
and look to destroy
all other seeds
attempting
to take
root.

Proverbs 11:2

*After pride came, disgrace followed;
but wisdom came with humility.*

James 4:6

*But he gives greater grace. Therefore it says:
"God opposes the proud, but he gives grace to
the humble."*

Matthew 23:12

*And whoever exalts himself will be humbled,
and whoever humbles himself will be exalted.*

Proverbs 16:18

*Pride goes before destruction,
and a haughty spirit before a fall.*

A re you
R eally trying to
R aise your status with prideful
O bedience to Almighty
G od? Don't you realize he
A lready knows that
N o one
C an be perfect
E xcept for him?

coming undone

i have sinned
before God
and man,
but my sin
before man
was because of
my sin before God.

my pride went,
and i fell,
and i'm afraid
i may never rise again.

Selections from Psalm 51

Look, I was guilty of sin from birth, a sinner the moment my mother conceived me. Cleanse me with hyssop and I will be pure; wash me and I will be whiter than snow. Grant me the ultimate joy of being forgiven. May the bones you crushed rejoice. Hide your face from my sins. Wipe away all my guilt. Create for me a pure heart, O God. Renew a resolute spirit within me. Do not reject me. Do not take your Holy Spirit away from me. Let me again experience the joy of your deliverance. Sustain me by giving me the desire to obey. Then I will teach rebels your merciful ways, and sinners will turn to you. Then my tongue will shout for joy because of your righteousness.

O Lord, give me the words. Then my mouth will praise you. Certainly you do not want a sacrifice, or else I would offer it; you do not desire a burnt sacrifice. The sacrifice God desires is a humble spirit—O God, a humble and repentant heart you will not reject.

The Time Is Now
inspired by Nancy DeMoss Wolgemuth's Seeking Him *study*

The time has come
to break it up,
the hardened soil
of the heart,

to humbly bow
before the Lord,
lest he condemn
and then depart.

The time has come
to bring a light
to secret sins
left in the dark,

to turn away
from sin's allure,
to make the contrast
clean and stark.

The time has come
to boldly go
and claim the power
of God's grace,

to strive for
holiness and act
as children of
his chosen race.

The time has come
to love the Lord,
whole-heartedly
his Word obey,

to keep the soul
and conscience clean
and rectify
without delay.

The time has come
to set those free
who've wronged us
(as we've wronged the Lord),

to live our lives
with purity,
rejecting selfish
sin's reward.

The time has come
to walk in step,
right by the Spirit's
guiding hand,

to gaze upon
the Lord each day
and study well
his sovereign plan.

*The time has come
to take your vow.
'Twill always be;
the time is now.*

follow

help
i begged give
me

change

to follow you

i thought i was trying
to show you Jesus
when really,
i was trying
to replace him.

—i'm an imposter

When Jesus said
that it was finished,
he didn't mean
except for me.

Convicted
a reflection on 2 Corinthians 9:7

*Each one must give
as he has decided in his heart,*

I only knew to give what
others decided for me.

*not reluctantly or
under compulsion,*

My service slowly became
hesitant and forced.

for God loves a cheerful giver.

All joy had been sucked
from my bones.

i didn't realize
that untruths
out of kindness
—*of course i can!*
no trouble at all!
i'd love to help!—
were actually lies.

—*a lie is a lie, no matter how kind*

surrender

harsh waves of realization
wash over my head,
threatening to drown,
unless i let them
do their work
of carrying me
back to shore.

waiting

i feel i have died
a thousand deaths
and am grateful
for the hope of a
future resurrection,
but what can i do now
in the burial?

reminder

Christ died and
was resurrected,
but he also stayed
a time in the ground.

so

i keep doing the work
that is right before me—
of listening and feeling
and being still,
until the day
my heart
beats fresh
again.

peeling therapy

she was so gentle in her peeling.
she could see to the center
even without a knife,
and certainly, she never used one.
just peeled the next thin layer
week after week after tear-filled week.

i kept thinking
that this was the week
of the final peeling, and
she would ask the next question,
and another layer would fall,
adding to the pile of
peels and tears.

More or Less

I couldn't make him love me more.
(Believe me when I say I tried.)
Through double dates
and filling plates
and vowing to be World's Best Mate,
I loved until I cried.

But

I couldn't make him love me more.
No matter how I'd idolize
my faithful acts and
filling cracks and,
"Please sit down, my dear; relax."
I started to despise.

And still

I couldn't make him love me more!
But then one day my soul transgressed.
I crashed and burned;
my spirit churned;
and yet he gave me love unearned.
My heart leapt dumbstruck when it learned—
       I couldn't make him love me less.

receiving

i learned to receive emotions,
not banish them like naughty children.
they may not tell the whole truth,
and they sometimes exaggerate,
but when they are ignored,
they sit and scream,
"PAY ATTENTION TO ME!"
until they explode.
or i do.

so i learned to hear them,
sit with them,
encourage them,
and bring them before
God my Father,
who made them all.
he helps us understand
each other and
guides me in the Truth.

> but i am not sure
> i will survive
> the intensity of
> these emotions.

learning to grieve

tears.
every day.
weeping, sobbing, whimpering.
headaches, puffy eyes, brain fog, silence.
spilling, leaking, dripping.
will it end?
wet.

A Lament

selections from Lamentations & the Psalms

It is said that

it is good to wait patiently for deliverance from the Lord.

But my heart no longer has any joy; my dancing has been turned to mourning. My heart is sick; I can hardly see through my tears. Panic and pitfall have come upon me, devastation and destruction. Streams of tears flow from my eyes, because I am destroyed. The waters were closing over my head. I thought I was about to die during this time of

waiting for deliverance from the Lord.

And yet death could not find me, for my tears showed that still I live! So why are you downcast, O my soul? Why so overtaken with grief? Is it not from the mouth of the Most High that everything comes—both calamity and blessing? Why should I complain when I am punished for my arrogance? Though he causes me grief, he then will have compassion on me, according to the abundance of his loyal love. For he is not predisposed to afflict or grieve his people. The Lord will not reject me forever.

It is good to wait patiently for deliverance from the Lord.

Let me sit alone in silence while the Lord is disciplining me; let me lift up my heart and hands to God in heaven; let me carefully examine my ways so I can return to the Lord. Bring me back to yourself, so I can return to you. Renew my life as in days before. I have called on your name, O Lord, from the deepest pit. You heard my plea: "Do not close your ears to my cry for relief!" You came near on the day that I called to you. You said, "Do not fear!" O Lord, you championed my cause; you redeemed my life, so that now I can say

it was good to wait patiently for deliverance from the Lord.

Psalm 27:13

Where would I be if I did not believe I would experience the Lord's favor in the land of the living?

weary

my eyes are tired of leaking
at every mention of your name.
to ache this deeply is exhausting—
a full ten minutes without pain
is cause for celebration,
but i have nothing left within me
to even start the dance.

no escape

i welcome sleep
for reprieve from my tears,
but even in my dreams,
i am drenched.

My Rain Cloud

My rain cloud is leaking.

I try to place buckets
strategically below,
but then unexpectedly,
there's a downpour—
the buckets are full;
the sidewalk is puddled;
and the innocent passersby
are sopping wet.

I apologize and
shake my head and
place No Walking signs
around the perimeter.

Most of the walkers obey.
A couple step in by accident
and feel the leaky drip drop,
drip drip, drop.

They look up at the cloud,
and it shakes under
the weight of the water
it fears to release.

Please go, it begs.
Please follow the signs.

They throw up their
umbrellas,
embarrassed to have
witnessed the struggle
of a weak cloud
that fills too quickly.

I step back in
to plug its holes,
to wrap some tarp
around its edges,
but it bursts again,
water flooding
the surrounding grass.

I try to distance myself
from the cloud,
pretend it doesn't
belong to me;
still with an eye out
to keep others safe and dry.

I call a cloud expert
to diagnose the issue.
I want to discuss it
outside the Wet Zone.
But she steps in
and looks up
and talks to the cloud.

My cloud looks at me,
confused.
No one has ever
talked to him or

asked him questions
or encouraged him to leak.

He holds himself a little tighter;
she seems too kind to get wet.
But she stays and
stays and stays,
and eventually, my cloud
begins to quiver.

I stand back,
knowing and afraid,
until it releases
its torrential rain.

But she doesn't run away.
She isn't afraid or
confused or disappointed.
With outstretched arms,
she begins to spin
and twirl and dance.

My cloud heaves and
releases the next layer
and the next and the next,
until the rain is no longer
in the cloud at all but
is pouring straight down
from the heavens,
right through its thin,
puffy frame.

And the cloud expert
keeps up her dance
all the while,
encouraging my cloud and
the rain and the storm.

I have never danced
in the rain before.
I have run away,
grabbed protective gear,
dashed through
to get to my house,
but never stayed out there
on purpose, to just be.

I place my hand
inside the Wet Zone
and withdraw it
to survey the damage.
Soaked.
But it doesn't hurt—
it is just wet.
So I place two hands in.
My arms follow.
A foot and a leg.
And before I know it,
I am surrounded.
It is warmer
than I'd expected;
softer, not piercing.

I begin to twirl,
to move with the rhythm
of the downpour.
A laugh escapes

through my lips.
I try to silence it,
but it is unavoidable—
I feel relief!
Not fear,
not embarrassment,
not shame.

We dance there,
the cloud expert and I,
until the rush slows
to a drip drip drop.
Then a drip, drop.

She embraces me,
wet and sopping,
without apology
and leaves,
offering to return
if he ever gets
plugged again.

Gets plugged?
But I plugged him!
I stopped him!
I shut him up!
To protect the others.
To protect myself.

But withholding doesn't
allow space for nature—
for cycles of receiving
and releasing.

I was the one
who was hurting
my poor cloud.

I glance up at him, but he
can barely see me through
his beaming smile.
I love to see him so happy.
I love to feel so free.

So I discard my signage and
let him leak and burst
whenever he needs.

And I always
stand close by
so I can join him
and dance
in the rain.

from me to me

don't dry your tears, darling;
they are washing away the pain.
don't stand up yet, sweetheart;
the weight is too much strain.
don't look around now, honey,
for the people you need to serve.
you have to spend some time right here;
deep in your heart, observe.

don't cover it up, baby;
the wound needs air to heal.
don't be afraid, my angel;
there's a lot of things to feel.
don't keep it inside, cupcake;
there are people you can trust
who are worthy to help you carry this load.
please let them in; you must!

there, there, now, little princess,
and doesn't that feel good?
come on downstairs, my dear one;
you have been understood.
the past won't leave you, sweetie,
but we'll all be right here.
and most important, God above
has drawn you very near.
you can stand strong on his true words;
you have no more to fear.

Thankfulness: An Unusual List

Pain,
tears,
anxiety,
fears.
Heart racing,
mind pacing—
all unknowns
this year.

Grief,
ache,
how much can
hearts take?
Old mourning,
new forming—
all done for
my sake.

All
this
is my thankful
list.
Christ molding,
never scolding—
'tis his faithful
kiss.

chapter five

Floating

Reading for Healing

I read for healing—

books on
anxiety,
best selves,
boundaries,
childhood,
codependency,
grief,
lament,
love,
mind-body connection,
personalities,
shame,
surrender,
vulnerability—

when suddenly,
for the first time
I recognized an untruth,
sitting there before my eyes,
about to feed my heart,
and shuddered at the amount
I had consumed,
begging it all to fill
every gaping hole,
never once considering
it might not be the first kind
of nutrition
I should ingest.

So for one year,
I stood up,
shook all helps from my healing heart,
put them high on a shelf
to be sorted through later,
and soaked myself in God's book,
the Bible,

because

Every scripture is inspired by God and useful for teaching, for reproof, for correction, and for training in righteousness.

and

The grass withers, the flower fades, but the word of our God will stand forever. (ESV)

and

Every word of God proves true; he is a shield to those who take refuge in him. (ESV)

I returned to the other books eventually,
and they were helpful
and healing,
but God is my teacher everlasting;
his Word is my faithful guide.

saved

i am looking to Jesus,
the light of the world,
the author and finisher
of my faith,

for there is no other name
under heaven given among men
by which i can be saved.

inadequacy
felt in myself is where Christ's
sufficiency reigns.

Psalm 90:14-17 (NIV)

Satisfy us in the morning with your unfailing love that we may sing for joy and be glad all our days. Make us glad for as many days as you have afflicted us, and for as many years as we have seen trouble. May your deeds be shown to your servants, your splendor to their children. May the favor of the Lord our God rest on us; establish the work of our hands for us—yes, establish the work of our hands!

the difference

my motive for serving
was not love
but fear of losing love.

we are made to
love one another,
not *be* one another.

The Best Samaritan

The Good Samaritan had boundaries.
Listen in—I'll tell you more,
because he was my greatest example
of putting others' needs before
my own. But then I read the story again
in my Bible I knew so well.
And I saw that, indeed, he carried him far
and paid for his stay, but what's bizarre
is that I never noticed he didn't dwell.
He went on his way and wished him well
and only returned to pay the bill,
but I hadn't seen that part until—
I'd picked up and carried and fed all his kids,
offered great counsel and sorted all lids,
purchased new housing and clothing amid
trying to keep my own family alive,
and slowly, but surely, I started to die.
Still I stomped and kept helping,
since I knew I could be
the BEST Samaritan
with no need for boundaries.

In the end, I was the body
on the side of the road,
and I have much still to learn
of all the things that I "know."

Layers of Healing

By my silent meditations,
        I   am   healed.

By my reading integrations,
        I   am   healed.

By my counselor consultations,
        I   am   healed.

By my friends and conversations,
        I   am   healed.

But then my learning takes a turn;
my understanding now discerns
that where my very soul's concerned,
it's only by my Savior's wounds that
        I   am   healed.

hindsight

you don't realize
how sick you are
until you are being made
well.

Reborn

My son cried
upon entering this side
and leaving the only home
he had ever known.

He wailed his plight
at blinding light,
this new heavy weight
and racing heart rate.

He was scared and hungry,
a boy without a country,
certain that he
was alone, not freed.

His screams nearly blocked
the comfort that rocked
and tried to soothe
this inconsolable youth,

that tried to assure him
this new life would mature him,
a place with space
to breathe and stretch at his own pace

and to become himself full-grown
in a way he had never known.

When he was born, my son cried,
and when God saved me,
so did I.

I AM NOT A VICTIM

I AM NOT A VICTIM.
I get to speak for me
and make it clear
I do not fear
what expectations be.

I AM NOT A VICTIM.
My choices shout out loud.
My yes is mine;
my no's not blind.
I'm rising tall and proud.

I AM NOT A VICTIM.
In this, I find some rest:
I stand before
a holy Lord;
he knows my very best.

Re-Entry

I knew it was time,
but I was feeling so scared.
There were people to talk to;
I wasn't prepared—

afraid that my pain
would spill over on them;
was it really the time
to invite them back in?

And then I came up
with the perfect solution:
they'd come over to sing,
and my contribution

would be playing piano
(and thus facing the wall).
The words would be printed there;
I wouldn't bawl.

So over they came,
and we said our hellos;
then down we all sat
with our babes and our phones

(to remember the words).
And we sang and we sang.
And I still faced that wall,
and still they all came,

month after month
for over a year.
And then one day I realized
where once had been fear,

a small hope had grown,
my love had renewed.
And then   I   turned   around   (!)
and shared my gratitude

and a bit of my story,
why I had invited—
it wasn't because I was
people-excited,

but rather, because
I knew deep in my heart
that to live around people
but never take part

was not the whole life
I had been called to live.
I had to step out,
though I could only give
a very small bit.

And yet they accepted,
and the growth in my heart
was more than I'd expected.
And I finally began
to feel re-connected.

And there in the end,
we all were affected,
because one person reached out
and was not rejected.

To Versus For

I am responsible to you—
        to love you,
        to serve you,
        and even
        to forgive you.

But

I am not responsible for you—
        your responses,
        your actions,
        your decisions,
        and retractions.

Those Great (Awful) Expectations

The thing I'm fearing most today
is not meeting others' expectations.
I'm afraid no matter what I do and say,
I'm causing someone great frustration.

I tried to learn to think of it all—
every future possibility—
plan accordingly each protocol,
feign an excessive heart of humility.

But something I'm learning in all of my planning
is that when I spend so much prep time obsessing,
I'm actually purposefully sitting there fanning
the pride in my heart and my self-centered guessing.

So I'm trying to learn to state what I'm willing
and able to do on my end of the deal,
and I'm hoping I'll find it much more fulfilling
than constantly dreading how others will feel.

Fences Make Great Boundaries

Fences make great boundaries
for people who are weak.
I don't need a fence to guard;
I'll turn the other cheek.

But what happens when you're weary,
and there's poop filling your yard?
And you realize that you welcomed it
from having no safeguard.

And now you're hiding in your house,
because you have no space
that's really only yours alone.
And so now you must face—

the people you've allowed to use
your property at whim
and must begin constructing walls;
the outcome's looking grim.

And grim it is at first because
it's a hard thing to undo—
the habit you've allowed to grow,
like where they place their poo.

But eventually your fence is built;
your yard is safe to walk.
And friends are welcome at your place,
provided that they knock.

holding pattern

i was holding onto Jesus
the best way i knew how—
through laws to be kept
and traditions to be upheld.
i gripped them firmly to my chest
and clung to them for life.

but when God
loosened my hold by
removing my strength,
i didn't even know
where Jesus was,
until i looked down
and saw myself secure
in the palm of his hand—
with nothing in mine.

credit

he has held me fast.
he does hold me fast.
he will hold me fast.

déjà vu

i met someone today who scared me.
she reminded me of past times
and people i once knew.

i tried to be brave and engage,
but i know the signs far too well
(both hers and mine),
and i had to walk away,
trembling and breathing prayers.

i guess i still have work to do,
and maybe i feel discouraged,
but at least i can sense what i need
and no longer play the victim.

using my tools

practicing my breathing,
helpful thinking,
out-to-friend reaching,
walking and talking,
up-to-God praying,
truths and lies weighing,
gonna get through this
panic attack.

practicing presence

i *feel* heart pounding and offer it a few long, slow breaths as weighted blanket presses me deeper into warming sheets.

i *hear* furnace engage as it sends a blast of heated air up through bedroom floor, listen to my husband's rhythmic breath as he enters sleep, try to borrow some of his peace.

i *watch* blurry shadows fade as my eyelids fall shut, pause images of the day, interrupt worries of tomorrow, let darkness tuck me in.

i *whisper* prayers to my father: *i love you, i trust you, please help me.*

i am here; i am now; i am present.

the battlefield of healing

healed is not perfection.
healed is not completion.
healed is not never
        warring in your mind or
        wavering in belief or
        struggling to stand strong
        in your newly adopted way of peace.
healed is recognizing darkness
and picking up your weapons
to fight.

Chew Your Fears

I swallow anxiety whole,
wash it down with a full glass of denial,
let it land in the pit of an unsuspecting stomach,
another *I'm fine* pressing the boulder further down.
But I don't account for the body's rejection
of such a concentrated substance, and suddenly
feel it ricocheting through my heart, until
the choking forces me to leave the table.

Its second appearance is even more fiercely solid,
and I stare, uncertain what to do with it.

I carry it delicately to a friend
who has a heart full of shareable tools.
We lay it out on the table,
begin to pick and pull and chisel apart
this thing that is mine, until each piece
is bite-sized and easier to digest.
She pours warm love and acceptance,
sprinkles reminders of truth,
and hands me a spoon.

No heavy stones, no rushing, no choking.
Just peace flowing gently through my insides.

Put It Out

Fear begins as a spark,
continued thought fans the flame,
dwelling hard burns the heart,
speaking it out opens the pane,
filling room with oxygen,
heightening fire, disguising shame.

But

soothing, calming, truth-filled, gracious,
peace-making, comforting, Spirit-skilled, audacious
words spoken back pour cooling water
on dying soul and working harder
douse the fire into embers—
sizzling sounds of peace, surrender.

Dear Mind,

Please don't shoot me! Don't get mad at me! Don't deny me or ignore me or shove me into a corner to never deal with again. I know you're afraid of the news I bring, but I'm just the messenger. You'll have to take it up with your heart.

Sincerely,
Your Emotions

course corrections: two

hands on steering wheel,
eyes on road.
calmly progressing,
slight adjustments
to stay in lane
(and not because
i've made a mistake,
necessarily).
occasional obstacle
startles, but
quickly get back
on course.
it still takes effort
and intentionality,
but i no longer
panic with every bump.

2 Corinthians 12:7b–10

So that I would not become arrogant, a thorn in the flesh was given to me, a messenger of Satan to trouble me—so that I would not become arrogant. I asked the Lord three times about this, that it would depart from me. But he said to me, "My grace is enough for you, for my power is made perfect in weakness." So then, I will boast most gladly about my weaknesses, so that the power of Christ may reside in me. Therefore, I am content with weaknesses, with insults, with troubles, with persecutions and difficulties for the sake of Christ, for whenever I am weak, then I am strong.

blessed wound

thorns prick and protect,
as much gift as they are curse,
    for
        they
  slow
      us
          down.

All-Sufficient Grace

My grace is sufficient
for you in your weakness,
and in fact, it's in
weakness I shine.

I may not remove
that which you disapprove,
but you need not
despair, mope, or whine.

Instead, be content
with the season I've sent,
with frailty and troubles
and stresses.

For the power of Christ
and his love sacrificed
are revealed in
lamentable messes.

Every Time

Every time my soul is rocked
and fears rise to the top,
I have a chance to turn to Christ—
in him, my fears are stopped.

Every time my heart is tossed
and pleasing man comes first,
I have a chance to look to Christ—
he can, my angst, reverse.

Every time my mind is pricked
and old thoughts come anew,
I have a chance to cling to Christ—
he is my staying glue.

So every time I flounder
and I feel despair begin,
I'll rejoice that I can dwell with Christ—
for his Spirit lives within.

My Sacrifice

I've long heard the phrase "a sacrifice of praise,"
and I'm trying to raise my hands.

But my heart sinks low; it is heavy and slow,
since I hardly know how to stand.

Then I think of the thing I can most surely bring
to the throne of my King with joy,

that which I've met that has daily beset
and has given me threats to destroy—

my anxiety, yes! It has made a great mess,
but can I use it to bless my Lord?

Well, it's all that I've got, and it won't be for naught,
so with that final thought I step toward

the One who's forgiven my heart's sin condition,
lay fear's disposition at his feet.

And I bow my head down without making a sound,
and my soul knew its Savior did meet.

Saying Goodbye to My Old Self

I've said goodbye to someone I knew very well,
someone I was comfortable with.

I didn't realize she kept hurting people
with her good intentions and by
denying her God-given limitations.

It doesn't matter anymore, because
God removed her from my life and
put someone new there.

She seems pretty timid, but
I think I'll learn to like her.

She's weaker, though perhaps steadier,
and she does look more like Jesus.

God's Peeling

God peeled the layers, one-by-one,
until I thought I'd come undone.

I felt such pain and wondered why
for me to live, I had to die.

He gently led me to the cross,
so I could name my aching loss

as gain!

And then his Spirit drew
my heart so close it became new.

And newness hurts! It's fresh and raw,
but God was with me and he saw

my every heartache, every fear,
and he collected every tear.

So now I can with sureness claim
that Jesus is my sweetest gain.

Acceptance

If God
who is infinite
has boundaries,
then surely I
who am finite
must.

freedom || boundaries: take four

hey God,
someone needs help,
and my heart feels heavy for her.
is this one of the good works that you've
prepared beforehand for me to do?
i know it's not my deeds
that make you love me,
and i know you can help her
even without me.
i'll check my heart
with your Spirit and Word
and my calendar with my husband
before i answer with my
impulsive self-sufficiency.
thanks for giving me access
to your Wisdom.

Paul and All

Paul didn't ask to be saved.
He was out "serving God"
but was really depraved—
to his laws and traditions
was fully enslaved,
>   and still
>   he didn't ask
>   to be saved.

Paul didn't ask to be blinded.
He was off on the road
and was feeling high-minded,
when the force of the Light
and the Lord's harsh words grinded,
>   and then
>   he was standing there,
>   blinded.

Paul didn't ask for correction.
He was sure he was right,
walking life with perfection,
when Jesus called out
gave his heart new direction,
> even though
> he didn't ask
> for correction.

God doesn't wait for our asking.
When we're dead in our sins
and don't care and sit basking,
he comes and he calls us
and starts the unmasking.
> So I'm thankful that God
> doesn't wait
> for our asking.

Psalm 34

I will praise the Lord at all times; my mouth will continually praise him. I will boast in the Lord; let the oppressed hear and rejoice. Magnify the Lord with me. Let's praise his name together. I sought the Lord's help and he answered me; he delivered me from all my fears. Those who look to him for help are happy; their faces are not ashamed. This oppressed man cried out and the Lord heard; he saved him from all his troubles. The Lord's angel camps around the Lord's loyal followers and delivers them. Taste and see that the Lord is good. How blessed is the one who takes shelter in him. Remain loyal to the Lord, you chosen people of his, for his loyal followers lack nothing. Even young lions sometimes lack food and are hungry, but those who seek the Lord lack no good thing. Come, children. Listen to me. I will teach you what it means to fear the Lord. Do you want to really live? Would you love to live a long, happy life? Then make sure you don't speak evil words or use deceptive speech. Turn away from evil and do what is right. Strive for peace and promote it. The Lord pays attention to the godly and hears their cry for help. But the Lord opposes evildoers and wipes out all memory of them from the earth. The godly cry out and the Lord hears; he saves them from all their troubles. The Lord is near the brokenhearted; he delivers those who are discouraged. The godly face many dangers, but the Lord saves them from each one of them. He protects all his bones; not one of them is broken. Evil people self-destruct; those who hate the godly are punished. The Lord rescues his servants; all who take shelter in him escape punishment.

From Life to Death to Life

The flower thought herself beautiful
perched there upon that limb.
She didn't know she soon would fall;
she just loved looking prim.

But one day as she fluttered,
dainty petals in the breeze,
she gasped as one began to float
down right below the tree.

As she clutched her petals tighter,
they each began to fall,
and she lay bare, and suddenly
felt, oh, so very small.

Poor Flower could not know
that the worst was yet to come,
for next she found herself afar
way down from cherry plum.

She hit the ground and shuddered,
not knowing what had occurred,
except that she was dying,
and then   —   her final stir.

The ground climbed over her body
and pulled it down in death,
and there she stayed all winter,
while springtime held its breath.

Our little flower was surprised
that she was now a seed—
her bottom taking root,
while her top pushed up through weeds.

She couldn't tell quite why
but her face longed for the Sun.
And she spent all her days
gazing only at that One.

She grew each day a little more—
the outside and within—
and was one day reminded
of the heights that she had been,

when she saw a struggling flower
on her own branch down below.
She spoke her kind, encouraging words
of *trust* and *let it go*.

And then at last, she saw herself
as she was meant to be—
not delicate pretty flower,
but deep-rooted, growing tree.

Happy Sad

I'm smiling more.
It's not fake,
but I'm also not
happy,
exactly.

My husband is encouraged
that healing is happening,
until I mention that
I still cry
every day,
and he is alarmed.

But I am not.

I don't feel depressed.
Every tear is expelling
some pain
or sorrow,
like taking the
World's Longest Shower—
I am becoming clean.

The Wound

The wound was deep,
took years to finally scab over,
until it was healed enough that
I no longer needed the bandage and
wasn't very careful with it and
had no pain.

But then someone came and picked off the
scab, and it started bleeding all over again.

I panicked.

Am I going back to then and there?
Am I in for years more before it will heal?
Will I ever be able to touch that spot and
not flinch in fear of pain?

I glanced down, anxious and saw—
a new scab forming. Already!

This wasn't regression.
It just needed a little bandage
and a little time,
and I was willing to give it

                                        both.

Peace Floats

You start with the swimming,
which is to say you start with the striving—
      the doing, the proving,
      the obsessive conniving
      of showing no weakness or
      slight limitation,
      the no-never-resting,
      the elusive foundation
      just barely surviving,

until you realize you're drowning,
which is to say you are losing your sureness—
      your peace and your footing and
      always-say-yes-ness.
      Identity's crumbling,
      new fears overtaking,
      and the depths of unlearning
      leave you breaking and shaking,
      while your hope fades in protest.

But you feel next the rescue,
which is to say that someone is listening—
      they see you and hear you, and
      they're not safely distancing.
      They're holding space open
      to give room for healing,
      and they never show fear at
      the darkness of feelings.
      They just stand there witnessing,

until your soul begins weeping,
which is to say you are now understanding—
>   this pain that's wreaked havoc
>   has been slowly expanding.
>   There's a whole different way
>   you are meant to be living.
>   Bow head in repentance;
>   feel fresh the forgiving.
>   You are new and are standing.

You end with the floating,
which is to say you know now of resting—
>   of peace bringing stillness,
>   a pause to the testing.
>   You're waiting, not frenzied,
>   unhurried existence;
>   you learn how to serve *and*
>   to ask for assistance
>   in soulful investing.

writing for healing

the words came pouring out.
i was purging my mind
of fear and shame
and sadness.

—let them come

done (for now)

i take a cleansing breath;
there's nothing left to say.
the words have tumbled out the door;
God's Word reached in, heart to restore;
together now, i need no more;
they've washed my fears away.

EPILOGUE

Redeemed II

The beauty of a body is that its many parts work together for one purpose—to walk, to cook, to create, to serve. But sometimes little pinkies get to thinking the foot could use some help to go faster, and really, they'd make a much better mouthpiece, and *have you seen how the eyes are so slow to spy the need right in front of them*, and so, said little pinky tries to juggle gripping and running and encouraging and noticing— all wonderful deeds, but only one of which she was designed to do. The other members of the body scoot out of her way and wander about, waiting for an opportunity to do their jobs. In the meantime, the pinky scurries in an alarming frenzy, all the while growing bitter and resentful, so that she eventually collapses in a fit of exhaustion and frustration, wondering *why no one else does anything around here* and *why is it always up to me* and *when will somebody finally notice all the good that I've done!* And in that collapse, the body will continue to walk and to cook, to create and to serve, and they'll wrap that little pinky gently and allow her to rest and to heal without condemnation or judgment. They'll call a therapist, who will strengthen that finger in all the ways she was designed to function, and one day, she will stretch and test her strength in writing and bending and painting and stabilizing, and she'll feel proud to be contributing again in all the right ways. She'll cheer on the other members with relief and gratitude for their contributions and reflect on the beauty of a body that uses its many parts to work together for one purpose.

And she'll know she has been redeemed.

APPENDIX

things to do for your anxious friend:

1. pray for her
2. give her a hug
3. ask "how are you today?" (thinking through the past week/month is too overwhelming)
4. listen
5. offer compassion (not judgment)—even when you don't understand
6. don't be afraid of her tears
7. offer to play with her kids (she feels so guilty for not doing it as much right now)
8. bring her food (not coffee)
9. pray with her
10. send her a note that reminds her she is not forgotten (with Scripture is a bonus)

Note: these things will not fix your friend, but they will demonstrate Jesus's love to her.

things to do for your anxious soul:

1. breathe...deeply and slowly
2. recite memorized truth
3. pray
4. keep breathing
5. take a bath (with all the bubbles)
6. text a trusted friend how you're feeling
7. accept their love and prayers
8. ask your spouse/friend for a hug
9. go outside
10. read a book (out loud is best) to yourself or your children
11. move your body/go for a walk
12. put on real pants
13. drink a glass of water...then splash some on your face
14. say something nice to someone
15. breathe again

Note: these things will not fix you, but they will demonstrate Jesus' love to your own self.

ACKNOWLEDGMENTS

new birth

so many have
crouched around me
as i labored for
hours, days, years,
massaging my back,
consoling my cries,
offering water.
and now look,
i've birthed a book,
and they're still
here cheering:
you did it!

—*no, no,* ***we*** *did it*

Lyndsay, my first counselor who made me safe to feel and gave me hope.

James, who walked through my darkest of days without complaint, who encouraged me to write for personal healing first, and whose art perfectly captures the emotion I was trying to express—how lucky am I?

My earliest readers who told me that this was indeed a book and whose insight made it better: Sarah B, Anna W, Renee T, Tess K, Anna H, Pam B, Bethy H, Becca G, Angela G, Amy E, Angie L, Monica B, Esther W, Jessica M, Lyndsay M, Ashlea M, BJ D, Alisha R, Lydia H, Claudette T, Bethany T, Taylor R, Amy S, Heidi J, Matthew H, Ashley W, Jenni H, Teah D, and Laura H.

Mary Vesperman, whose editing wizardry has turned my stone into a gem.

PREVIOUSLY PUBLISHED

"exhausted." (Former title "wearing down.") *Carolina Muse*. 9 April 2022. pg. 12.

"unplanned guide." "Dayenu." "On Meditation." "Put It Out." "More or Less." *Agape Review*. 26 February 2023.

"From Life to Death to Life." "The Journey." *The Way Back to Ourselves*. 2 April 2023.

"faulty interpretation." "the best samaritan." *The Way Back to Ourselves*. July 2023.

"black hole." *Vessels of Light*. 15 July 2023.

"the helper's high." "obsessed." "if an addict." "obligations." "Those Great (Awful) Expectations." *The Way Back to Ourselves*. August 2023.

"reborn." *Awake Our Hearts*. 17 September 2023.

"The Battlefield of Healing." "Happy Sad." *The Way Back to Ourselves*. 28 Nov 2023.

"Paul and All." *Modern Reformation*. January 2024.

AUTHOR BIO

Sarah Steele is a poet and lifelong teacher. These days, that looks like leading her four lively redheads in their Michigan homeschool and engaging with students of all ages in poetry workshops, watercolor classes, nature studies, Bible discussions, and neighborhood book clubs.

You can find Sarah's poems in many publications, including *The Way Back to Ourselves,* where she is an editor. She has published two alphabet books with her graphic designer husband (yes, also a redhead). This is her first book for grownups.

Visit Sarah's website for free resources and more info: **bysarahsteele.com**.

Visit Sarah's Etsy shop for poetry and watercolor art: **bysarahsteele.etsy.com**.

www.ingramcontent.com/pod-product-compliance
Lightning Source LLC
Chambersburg PA
CBHW070422010526
44118CB00014B/1868